Bobbin's Story

as told to

one of the ladies

she 'owns'.

Bobbin's Story
by Brenda Cashford

This book was first published in Great Britain in November 2010
by Coast and Country Publications, Tyldesley House,
Clarence Road, Llandudno, Conwy LL30 1TW.
Tel 01492-870883.

www.coastandcountrymagazine.co.uk

www.ebookexchange.co.uk

Published, promoted & distributed by
Coast and Country Publications Ltd.

This paperback edition was first published in November 2010.
Text © by Brenda Cashford.
Photographs © by Brenda Cashford.

The moral right of Brenda Cashford to be identified as author of this work has been asserted by her in accordance with the Copyright, Designs and Patents Act 1988.

All rights reserved. No part of this book may be reproduced or utilized in any form or by any means, electronic or mechanical, including photocopying, recording or by any information storage or retrieval system, without permission in writing from
Coast & Country Publications.

A catalogue record for this book is available from the British Library.
Paperback edition ISBN 978-1-907163-34-0

Bobbin's Story

When I was a very tiny little kitten, about six weeks old I think, I was given to an old lady who had never had a pet before (her friends thought a little girl kitten would be company for her). It seems that she did not really know what a tiny kitten needed and I was rather naughty, running up her curtains, scratching her furniture and behaving like a normal kitten.

She did not know how to deal with me so tied a piece of string round my neck and the other end to a table leg, she also did not know that I needed good food and fed me on scraps so I was a rather small, unhappy kitten. The string round my neck was hurting my voice and in the end I had no meow; I could purr but not make any other sounds.

After several weeks the lady decided she could not keep me and sent me to the vet to have me 'put to sleep'. There a kind lady took pity on me and found someone to give me a loving home. This is the story of my life so far.

When I arrived at my new home I found I 'owned' one lady person, one gentleman person and another lady person who lived in her own flat in the house, also another lady and gentleman who visited very often.

At first I was kept away from the other animals in the house, this was until I had got used to my new surroundings, also I had rather a lot of nasty biting things in my rather thin fur. The gentleman person spent hours combing me until I was clean again but my poor neck had suffered badly from the string, (I had no fur on my neck and this took a long time to recover.)

After a few weeks of lovely food, loving care and playthings I was much more as a kitten should be, my favourite toys being empty cotton reels which I used to chase round the floor until I could catch them and KILL THEM. It was my liking for these playthings which suggested a name for me - BOBBIN.

Soon after I arrived at my nice new home I nearly lost one of my nine lives, it happened like this. My 'people' went away for a holiday and the 'visiting lady and gentleman' came to look after us, us being myself, the two dogs, another cat, the doves and various wild animals that live in the grounds around the house. They were asked to visit me often in my special room (it was really the kitchen of the lady who had the flat, she was away staying with other members of the family for Christmas) so I didn't get too lonely. The visiting lady came to see me often, brought my food, brushed me and played with me.

One day I decided to play a prank on her when she came to see me. She could not find me so sat down in the armchair and called me only to leap up in the air - I was under the cover (it was an old sheet really, put there so I didn't spoil the chair) and she sat on me. The lady was very upset because she thought she had squashed and hurt me so I rushed about playing with my cotton reels just to show I was fine. I heard the lady telling the gentleman what had happened and how upset she was, he came to have a look at me and said I was OK and not to worry.

In time I was allowed to meet the other animals. There was a big black dog called Cassie, a black and white collie called Tammy and another cat - quite old I think - called Minky. Eventually we all became friends, (although I'm sure Minky got fed-up with me jumping on her!)

Another big black dog (she was Cassie's sister) visited us quite a lot with the visiting lady and gentleman, her name was Emma and she adored me. Emma would sit for ages just watching me and follow me wherever I went.

Emma sitting gazing at me, I often smacked her face with my paw but she did not mind.

Nearly another life gone.

Life went on happily until I was about six months old when I nearly lost another of my nine lives. I had a terrible accident. One Tuesday evening I decided that the garden was not exiting enough and jumped over the wall to explore further. Goodness knows what hit me but Oh! it did hurt. After a long time I managed to get back into the garden and started to drag myself through the bushes. I could hear them calling me but because of my damaged voice I couldn't cry out to let them know where I was. Our garden is full of rhododendron bushes that animals can get through but not humans therefore my people could not search properly and find me.

After being missing for five days I somehow managed to drag my poor body home, neither I nor anybody else knows how I managed it or how I got through the cat-flap, this has a high step to reach it, but I knew I had to do it for myself.

My gentleman had gone to check the back door was locked for the night, (I heard him say although he was sure it was locked something made him check again) and found me leaning against the washing machine.

I was exhausted and when he picked me up realised I had been very badly hurt and although nearly midnight on a Sunday he telephoned for the vet who came immediately. She examined me and said I had a broken pelvis, (when they x-rayed me they found it was broken in three places) and a fractured back leg and starving; I hadn't been able to eat or drink for five days, so I was taken to surgery. After three days "tender loving care" I was strong enough to have an operation to mend my broken bones. After I returned home many weeks went by with lots of love and careful nursing. Emma and her owners came often and Emma lay in front of me, gazing anxiously at me as usual where I was lying on my cushion, I was really rather enjoying all the fuss being made of me. When I did manage to walk I looked very sad but also funny because my back leg had no fur, (they had to shave it for the operation) and I walked lopsided but I was young and was looked after by my people so well that I made a complete recovery. You should see me go up the tall pine tree in the garden, it does frighten the birds and worries the squirrels a lot too.

Here I am completely recovered

One thing that emerged from my ordeal is that foxes do not seem to attack cats because, although I was really helpless for five days the foxes that live in the area did not touch me. I have grown into a beautiful cat, a very 'chocolate box' cat, everybody says so - including myself. My coat is a long silky brown and I have a bushy tail which I carry straight up in the air when I run to make a fuss of people I like!

I'm not a 'cuddly' cat as I do not like being picked up and will not sit on any laps, I will rub round the legs of people I know and like and have been known to give ankles a little nip, just to show I care.

*L*ife went on in this blissful way with me getting into all sorts of scrapes and being in trouble for tormenting Minky and for catching birds, (surely that is what cats are meant to do!)

I could always make Minky move off her chair just by looking at her.

The lady who comes to look after us when our people go away has nicknamed  me "The Monster", I can't think why. I wonder if it could have been because I caught a little wren who had become quite tame?

When I was about two years old something very strange happened to the garden. I went out through the cat-flap and the ground was covered in cold white stuff, the like of which I had never seen before. Walking very carefully I explored and found I did not like it very much, it stuck to my fur and made my paws cold.

The silly dogs loved it and rushed about the garden grabbing lumps of it in their mouths, chasing each other and rolling over and over. As soon as I could I went indoors where I was given a nice rub down with a warm towel, they had quite a job getting the snow lumps out of my chest fur!

*L*ife had been very good, I was fit again and was able to explore and go hunting, suddenly everything was not so good; first my good friend Emma became very ill and in May went to the place all of us go, the ''Animal Heaven' A few weeks later Cassie was taken ill and she joined her sister Emma in the 'Animal Heaven'. This meant that Tammy, Minky and myself were left.

*E*veryone seemed sad and we all missed the dogs so my people decided they would get two more big dogs. They were not very big when they arrived, not much bigger than me so I soon put them in their place. They have been called Poppy, who is chocolate brown and Cassie Two who is black like the first Cassie.

This is Poppy   and this is Cassie Two

Waiting for dinner

I was very surprised how quickly they grew into big dogs but I made them understand, "I am boss and you do not mess about with me," They are my friends now and when I come in from a busy night hunting they clean my ears for me.

Cassie Two and Poppy when they grew up

*T*here is one thing Cassie and Poppy will insist on doing and it is this, when I am having a lovely sleep they fly up barking and nearly frighten the wits out of me which makes me run in terror. I know they like to announce that a car has come up the drive or someone has rung the doorbell but I do wish they would do it quietly!

*T*he lady and gentleman who lived with Emma will not have anymore pets but will share all of us and they come to look after us when our people go on holiday.

One hot August afternoon I was having a wonderful time trying to catch the goldfish in the pond, (I must confess I have caught a few in my time). The 'visiting' lady was sitting reading on the veranda when all of a sudden I leaned too far and overbalanced and fell headfirst into the pond, the lady jumped up but before she could reach the pond I was out of the water and only the tip of my tail was wet. The lady realised this was not the first time I had fallen in! I walked away with as much dignity as I could muster and tried to pretend nothing much had happened.

Where we live is home to many kinds of wild animals and I am by nature a hunter so our paths cross quite a lot. We have a mutual respect for one another and I love to watch quietly from the top of the fishpond when the badgers and foxes come to the lower lawn to feed. I'm sure they know I'm there but they ignore me and get on with their supper.

I'm sure if my people knew the adventures that befell me in the wild land around they would be very worried about me, one thing I do know is I know how to look after myself and take great care not to annoy anyone else.

When I was very small pretending to be a big fierce animal

A very interesting thing happened one day, in the garden we have a bothy (this is a shed or store built of local stone). The lawnmower lives there with other garden tools. Suddenly my 'gentleman' and the 'visiting gentleman' worked very hard making it safe for someone.

Of course I had to go and find out what was going on and wonder of wonders, inside were lots of white birds (I found out later they were doves). My appearance at the wire netting door sent them into a frenzy.

The doves all calm before I appeared at the door

It was great fun although my gentleman seemed cross with me, can't think what I have done wrong? I spent hours trying to find a way in but they had been too clever for me and made it too secure. One day I noticed at the side of the bothy there was a stack of logs, I climbed to the top and found a little gap I think I could have squeezed through but someone saw me so, I walked away pretending I was going to my secret place for a sleep. later, when I returned to the bothy the rotten things had moved the logs so I could not get up there. After that I spent hours near the door of the bothy hoping that someone would forget to shut it, sadly they never did.

Some weeks later the little trapdoor in the top of the wall was opened and after a time the doves ventured out to fly around, I spent hours jumping in the air trying to catch one, every time they flew out of my reach just as I got to them. I heard my people say that in the beginning there were 16 doves and now there were over 50 you'd think they would let me have just one, wouldn't you? After a while the bothy was not big enough for all the doves so my people had a new dovecote built for them, this is proving just as hard to get into, I've never managed it.

Some of the doves on the lawn

This is the new dovecote, it has a netting door too and I love to frighten them by looking in, that is all I can do.

One night, after I had finished hunting I brought a little mouse in as a present for my people, (I often do but they never seem very pleased about it). The silly little thing got into a panic and ran up inside the curtains between the lining and the fabric. Of course the stupid thing couldn't find its way out, I waited some time then got bored so I went to my bed. A day or two later I heard rather a lot of commotion and found that my mouse had chewed its way out of the curtains - right up near the rail leaving several holes. I was not popular I can tell you, those curtains were new and the holes were right where they could be seen!

I tried to tell them I had brought the mouse as a present but everyone seemed so cross they wouldn't listen. I did hear them saying it had cost a lot of money, (what ever that is) to put a new panel in the curtain. They do not seem grateful for presents. A few days later I heard my 'lady' asking if anyone wanted a cat, I wonder whom she meant?

During the summer I spend a lot of time in the great outdoors as there are so many things to hunt; not that I catch much. Our land is covered in rhododendrons and when I push through the undergrowth I get the sticky buds stuck in my fur. This I do not like, even less do I like anyone trying to get them out for me. I do not scratch or bite - just run away. What I much prefer is find a nice bed or armchair and snuggle down comfortably pulling the buds out one by one. It does make rather a mess I must confess and although they grumble a bit they let me do it my way.

*F*or many years, when anyone spoke to me I tried to answer but of course no sound came out until one day I went to the study where the 'lady who visits' was using the computer. I wanted some dinner so I opened my mouth and a funny little squeaky meow came out, The lady thought it was the chair squeaking and turned round to have a look, she saw me sitting there repeating the performance and although not a very forceful meow at least I can make people understand me. The lady did and she was so delighted she took me to the 'animal room' and gave me some special fish for my dinner.

*E*very day I visit the lady who lives in her own little flat as she gives me cheese which I love, last week I ate every bit she gave me and decided I wanted some more. I know where she keeps it so I went to the fridge and tried to reach the door handle but found I couldn't open it. It worked as the lady saw me and opened the door to get me another piece, people do spoil me but I do such funny things which make them laugh; such as sitting in the fruit bowl when it's empty.

One year when my people were away on holiday and the visiting 'lady and gentleman' were doing their 'animal sitting' we had another upsetting time. Three days after they left for their holiday Cassie was taken very ill, she was a naughty girl and would eat things she shouldn't when walking in the local forest. The vet seemed to think this is what she had done and whatever it was had been poisoned. She was taken to the dogs hospital for five days. Even I was distressed because I missed Cassie and everyone seemed so sad and worried. When Cassie was well enough to come home from the hospital she had to be given lots of 'tender loving care' and special food several times a day. We other animals thought this was a smashing idea and were sure we were going to be fed at the same time. It didn't work out like that as somehow they managed to give Cassie her extra food and keep it from us, I call that unfair.

By the time my people arrived home from their holiday Cassie, although not terribly well was a lot better, they continued with the special feeding and care and thank goodness she is back to her old self. In fact she is rather naughty because she found out, as I did when I was hurt, that our people spoil you a lot as they are worried and want to make you better.

We have had lots of ups and downs in our household during the years that I have lived here, animals have come for a while before going to other homes, one of the animals who came to stay for a while was a striped 'Boy' cat who was two years old and much bigger than me.

He did not mix with any of us, humans he liked but not other animals so he was given a bed in the garden room and only let out when we were all indoors. I hated him and told him so - if I got the chance.

The hope was that 'Boy' would get to like us and be able to live indoors with us all. The situation did not improve however and when he was allowed outside he stalked round the house looking in the windows 'swearing' at any animal he caught sight of, with me inside growling back at him. My 'lady' felt sorry for him so allowed him into the study, we other animals were not encouraged in there. The 'Boy' repaid this privilege by scratching the very nice sofa bed in there, my people covered it with an old duvet cover but he found his way under that and clawed the upholstery so he was banished to the garden room again.

There came a day when we were both outside but my people did not realise this. They were both in the lounge doing paper-work when from the front garden came the most appalling sound of an animal screaming.

At first it was thought some animal was being attacked and killed so they rushed outside with powerful torches and discovered the noise was coming from ME (how I managed to make such a dreadful noise I do not know, temper I expect). I had got 'Boy' up a corner and was telling him to go back where he came from because I hated him. My people picked me up and took me indoors, I was furious especially when they fixed the cat-flap so I couldn't get out. Eventually I did manage to get after him again and would go to the garden room and swear at him through the window. He would cower up the corner absolutely terrified of me, I fluffed up my fur and made myself look twice as big, I even went into the garden room after him if the window was open but I was quickly removed if anyone found me there which made me very cross.

This went on for some time and then 'Boy' got bolder and he would go through the cat-flap, past the dogs (the silly things were frightened of him and cowered in their beds) and into the house where he would attack poor Minky if he got the chance. They tried to prevent this as Minky was old and frail and couldn't put up much of a fight.

One day I was being my bold aggressive self when the 'Boy' realised he was bigger and stronger than me. Oh dear, did he beat the living daylights out of me? I was terrified and fled up my favourite pine tree where he did not follow me for which I was truly thankful.

When I could get away I managed to get indoors where I stayed, they bolted the cat-flap to stop him getting in because he had decided he could thrash me anytime he felt like it!!

For some time I dare not go outside, I even had to use my litter tray - which I do not like - because I was afraid to go out into the garden. My people were rather worried about me as I didn't seem very well.

In the end the 'Boy' was found another home as he did not like to share his domain with other animals and they were afraid he would find Minky on her own and that would be the end of her, also my life and that of the dogs was being made very unhappy.

'Boy' is now very happy as "King Cat" in his own territory with only stray cats to see off. So all's well that ends well. I don't think I could ever have got to like him anyway.

Not long after the 'Boy' episode poor Minky seemed to fade away and she joined Emma and Cassie One in the 'Animal Heaven'. I heard them saying she was at least 18 years old, that is in cat years but in human years it made her about 110. I was surprised how much I missed her but it is rather nice being the only cat. Although I am older and a bit more staid I still manage to get into trouble quite often.

As I said at the beginning of my story Tammy was here when I joined the household. Now she is a very old lady, my people say she is 14 years old, this is a good age for a collie it seems.

She sleeps a lot of the day but not very much at night. She keeps getting 'my lady' out of bed because she wants to make sure everybody is still there, after she is reassured she will go back to sleep but it makes the 'lady' very weary as she doesn't get much sleep.

One of the naughty things I do (I can't seem to stop myself as it is such fun) is creep up on Tammy when she is sound asleep and give her a nip on her back legs. I don't think I hurt her, just make her jump but I get shouted at if anyone sees me do it. Poor Tammy is very deaf so she does not know anyone is there until they touch her, this is why I get into so much trouble.

I know I am a very lucky little cat to find a home where animals are so welcome even when, like me they can be rather naughty at times.

This is my favourite secret place, my 'gentleman' found me one day and took my picture.

June 1995

*O*h dear, I've done it again. I was in my box not looking very well and my 'lady' was worried about me. She was also rather cross because she had seen me sitting near a mouse hole and thought I had eaten too many baby mice. What had really happened was I had jumped over the wall again and something hit me. This time I was able to get back indoors quite quickly after the accident. My lady went to take me out of my box and I'm afraid I growled at her. I was hurting so much I dare not let her pick me up.

*A*t this she was really worried and took me to the vet, a different lady vet this time but very nice, they still thought I was suffering from a tummy upset or had been in a fight with another cat. I had a small wound on the side of my face that made them think this. So, I had another needle popped into me to give me some antibiotics.

*A*fter another three days there was no improvement so back to the vet, this time they discovered I had another fracture of the pelvis (a different place from the other three fractures) and a torn ligament in my right back leg. They said they thought a vehicle of some kind had hit me. I tried to tell them that was what had happened!

*T*reatment prescribed was complete bed-rest for three weeks. At first it was easy to stay where I was as I felt so terrible nothing would make me come out of my carrying basket. The only time I dragged myself out was to use my tray - this did not happen very often. My 'lady and gentleman' went on holiday and the 'visiting lady and gentleman' came to look after

me, Poppy, Cassie, the house, the doves but not poor Tammy as old age had finally taken her to join her friends in that 'Animal Heaven' I have mentioned before.

*A*ll went well for the next few days, part of my treatment was I had to be fed on fresh fish - lovely, I really enjoyed this and I was given special cat milk, which I also love.

*T*he first morning of the 'visiting' lady's stay she brought me my fish and milk and stayed with me to make sure I was not lonely. I managed to get on her lap which really surprised her because I had never done so before but I did feel I needed a lot of 'tender loving care' and she gently smoothed my fur sending me to sleep. After about an hour she was getting a bit bothered as she had other chores to do but did not like to remove me from her lap. Soon though I had to get off as I moved my position and hurt myself. I retreated to my carrying basket and went to sleep, as the 'lady' said, 'Sleep is a great healer' and certainly I did a lot of that.

Things went on quietly for several days, me getting stronger each day, still limping badly but I found if I tucked my bad leg up I could run quite fast. I was allowed out into the rest of the house. Poppy and Cassie were so pleased to see me and were very gentle, not knocking me or rushing round the house, as they seemed to know I was not strong yet. I soon went back to my 'safe' area as I got very tired, very quickly.

My 'lady and gentleman' were due back from their holiday on the Friday and that day I was an absolute pest!!!!! I felt so much better I wanted to go outside but wasn't allowed to. Every time anyone opened a door I tried to get there first, if I managed it they dare not open the door for fear I would rush out. I went round all the windows to see if any were open so I could get out but, although it was a hot day no one had dared to open a window.

I was so cross at the end that I swore and growled at anyone who came near me, I suppose it was very naughty but I did want to go out so badly. When my 'lady and gentleman' arrived home I was so pleased to see them but they wouldn't let me out either!

After several days of trying to keep me indoors my 'lady' decided to let me take my chance outside. At first it was scary and I didn't stay out long but each day made a difference and now I'm outside most of the of the day. I still cannot manage the cat-flap so I have to climb up the garden gate, get onto a low roof and from there through the open bedroom window.

Of course I have to wake everyone to let people now that I'm safely in and if there is any food going I would like some, please. It is rather surprising but they do not seem at all pleased to see me. It is a puzzle to everyone - but not to me - how I can climb up to the window but not get through the cat-flap!?!

I'm still very beautiful and really grateful for all the care, attention and love I've received.

Perhaps one day I shall lose my limp but it really doesn't bother me much, I can still do all the things I enjoy such a frightening the doves by sitting outside their door, stalking the birds that come to feed at the bird tables and prowling about the grounds. Where do I go? - that is my secret.

Up-date.

Such a lot has happened since I last told the story of myself and all my animal and human friends I thought you would like to know how we are all getting on.

Last year Poppy became very ill and in the end she joined the others in the 'Animal Heaven'. I too was not well. I kept getting thinner and thinner even though I ate my dinner every day.

*M*y 'lady' took me to the vet who said I had some trouble with my kidneys. The treatment was an injection, this I did not like much and then I had to have some special food that I do like. No more fish which does not please me, still on the special diet food I have grown fat as butter and look better than I have looked for years. My coat is thick and glossy and my eyes bright. Chocolate Box cat again.

*A*fter Poppy left us to join the others in the 'Animal Heaven' Cassie was very sad and wouldn't do a lot except sleep in her bed, she also injured her leg very badly and had to have an operation, my people said this was not very successful and poor Cassie was often in pain. It was decided she needed a companion to 'buck her up' a bit, so, off they went to the animal rescue centre where they found a lady dog called (at this time) Sasha who had been found straying. After being in kennels for two months she had become very upset.

*W*hen she had been with the family for a while she was renamed Mango.

Mango on her sofa

I have never met Mango as my family have discovered she does not like cats!!?? We now live our lives separately, an arrangement that works perfectly.

*O*ne day as I came down stairs having had a nice sleep on the master bed, to my horror Mango was in the lounge, she rushed towards me but I froze on the stairs (with fright really) Mango couldn't understand this and stopped in her tracks then walked away. My 'lady' found her and took her into the kitchen so I made my escape through my new cat-flap which had been put in the front door.

*W*hen Mango had been with us 18 months; she had been a good companion to Cassie, but Cassie had now joined all the others in the 'Animal Heaven' . This leaves just Mango and myself and I spend most of my time asleep in my special bedroom, going out sometimes if I feel like it, life is not at all bad, in fact it is very good.

*A*s I have got older I have changed a lot, for one thing I love being groomed now, something I hated when I was younger, then I would not stay, always jumping down and running away when someone tried to brush and comb me. Also I will now climb on to special people's laps, only when I feel like it though.

*S*ince Mango has been on her own she has become very dependant on my 'people' and I've heard them discussing the possibility of companions for her.

Now I find they have been to the animal shelter and seen a black, tan and white collie cross, I believe she is called Minnie - soon to be Midgy as my people decided they didn't think Minnie suited her, Midgy will be coming to live with us soon.

This is

Midgy

Up-date 2002

Here we are in 2002 and I'm still going strong. I spend all of my time indoors now as I'm a very old lady. To date I have not 'officially' met Mango and Midgy as I am not strong enough to defend myself if necessary so I live in my special bedroom, I have a heated pad in my igloo which is lovely and cosy. I enjoy my special cat food and love being groomed

*B*obbin lived to the ripe old age of 16 which was amazing for a pussy cat who lost so many of her nine lives. We -even the dogs - missed her terribly when she joined all her friends in the Animal Heaven.

As Bobbin would of said,

"I had a lovely life and I was a very *LUCKY LITTLE CAT*"

Bobbin's Story was tested by the Junior School, Wirksworth, Derbyshire. The children loved it and looked forward to the next week's Story lesson. After the story was finished they wrote letters to me as part of their lesson giving their views, it was lovely to receive these.

We have found Bobbin's Story is an ideal first read by Mum's & Dad's and Grandparents.

          Brenda Cashford.